I0364593

_____ is

BECOMING
even more
COURAGEOUS

Mr. B

Becoming Even More Courageous
Star Character Series
Copyright © 2019 Matthew Baganz

All rights reserved, so yes, we welcome you to use this book or parts thereof to reproduce in any form, store in any retrieval system, or transmit in any form by any means—electronic, mechanical, photocopy, recording, or otherwise—without prior written permission of the publisher. You hearby have written permission. We get it. We're teachers too. Should you have any other inquiries or permission requests, please contact us at:

Liv & Blue Publishing, LLC
P.O. Box 321
Pewaukee, Wisconsin 53072-0321
USA
livandbluepublishing@gmail.com
www.livandbluepublishing.com

Although the author and publisher have made every effort to ensure that the resource information in this book was correct at time of press, the author and publisher do not assume and hereby disclaim any liability to any party for any loss, damage, or disruption caused by errors or omissions, whether such errors or omissions result from negligence, accident, or any other cause. Links to third party websites are provided by Liv & Blue Publishing, LLC in good faith and for information only. The publisher disclaims any responsibility for the materials contained in any third party website, application program, or other serivce referenced in this work.

Printed in the United States of America
For orders outside the United States, products may be printed in England, China, Germany, Italy, India, Poland, Russia, or South Korea.
ISBN: 978-1-7327463-3-6

Created by Matthew Baganz
Cover design based on concepts by Inspired Cover Designs
Graphic design editing by Michael Neon
Star characters by Tasnim Jad

The Theory of Multiple Intelligences (P99_118) was developed by Howard Gardner.

Unless otherwise stated, all images from Bigstock.com. Cover image: vitasunny (depositphotos.com); P3: Rido81; P3: digitalista; P4: Jakub Jirsak; P5: PixelsAway; P12_18, 25_27, 32_33, 46_47, 62_63, 70_71, 82_83, 130_131: clearviewstock; P12_13: JaySi; P14: booka1; P14: A.F. Bradley, New York; P14: Walter Albertin, World-Telegram; P14: chariserin (Flickr); P14: Adria Richards (Flickr); P14: Katrina Afonso; P14: S.macken6; P18: VectorPot; P18: anatolir; P18: youarehere; P18: Iraida_Bearlala; P18: Barmaleeva; P18: IIIerlok_Xolms; P18: Agor2012; P18: rodin_A; P18: normaals; P19: Taawon; P23, 68, 72, 95: Sunwards Art; P24: Cheremuha; P25: Elnur; P28: Next Mars Media; P29: senoldo; P33: Ket4up; P34: maurus; P34: kenny001; P34: MSSA; P34: SvitlanaNiko; P35: vectorfusionart; P35: Celso Pupo; P36, 44, 62: MicroOne; P37: escova; P37: Seamartini; P40: thailerderden10; P40: romantiche; P41: infadelus; P45, 108: Tropical studio; P45: AlexKozlov; P45: Rafael Ben Ari; P45: manes; P46: Ambassador80; P46_47: tuulijumala; P47: Kravtzov; P47: puhimec; P48: nicemonkey; P49: Vicheien Petchmai; P49: victorflowerfly; P49: Christian Baloga; P49: topten22photo; P50, 60, 73, 76, 110: Yastremska; P50: Jovani Carlo; P50: Billyfoto; P51: Pavel1401; P52: alexfiodorov; P53: nisara; P53: salajean; P56: Mirek Kijewski; P56: Life on White; P56: Petlin; P57: mathisa; P57: arbit; P57: Tawng; P58: stokkete; P59: N_Defender; P59: Kinek00; P59: robuart; P59: Veleri; P116: Mike_Kiev; P62: Flat_Enot; P63: PiLens; P63: Bill45; P66: Rido81; P67: BVT; P68: style-photographs; P69: Lopolo; P69: ober-art; P70_71: Maria_Savenko; P72: VaLiza14; P73: Victority; P76_P77: United Nations Sustainable Development Goals logo and 17 icons from https://www.un.org/sustainabledevelopment, ©2019 United Nations. Used with the permission of the United Nations; Mikhail Leonov; P78: Rawpixel.com; P79: Tartila; P80: orson; P81: AlexMax; P82_83: tshooter; P84: ADragan; P84: Olivier; P84: haveseen; P85: Macondo; P85: Sakuramos; P85: Rost-9; P86: Dikobraziy; P87: Fairtrade Mark; P90: AlexLMX; P91: Klavapuk; P92: Andrey Suslov; P93: WeVideo logo; P94: Jakub Jirsak; P96: Burdun; P97: aquir; P100: denisfilm; P100: www.BillionPhotos.com; P100: ruslan_shramko; P100: patiwat sariya; P100: igor stevanovic; P100: jgroup; P100: Rinderart; P100: AnnekaS; P100: maxxyustas; P102: Waldemarus; P102: Lopolo; P102: VectorKnight; P102: Dorian2013; P102: ilkercelik; P102: prometeus; P102: amorphis; P102: jr4jesus; P102: amiak; P104: thinglass; P104: lembergvector; P104: Alisen Anima; P104: rvlsoft; P104: Designer_things; P104: MrTwister; P104: volare2004; P104: Adam1975; P104: Inspired Cover Designs; P104: vitasunny (depositphotos.com); P104: Bigaurinko; P106: pdsci; P106: photoboyko; P106: abstract412; P106: Yourg; P106: N_Defender; P106, 112: egal; P106: Alex Staroseltsev; P106: Ulianna; P106: leungchopan; P108: sutthinon; P108: famveldman; P108: Tatyana_Tomsickova; P108: Paul Burns; P108: HighwayStarz; P108: vdovichenko; P108: yarruta; P108: filistimlyanin; P110: CreativePhotoTeam.com; P110: eamesBot; P110: undrey; P110: sasirin pamai; P110: Sergey Nivens; P110: sutthinon; P110: ijeab; P110: Javier Brosch; P112: OnlyZoia; P112: wittayayut; P112: LightField Studios; P112: BlueOrange Studio; P112: Anna Om; P112: .shock; P112: Rido81; P112, 114: monkeybusinessimages; P114: manushot; P114: lola_art; P114: fredleonero; P114: Alen Thien; P114: Davdeka; P114: pavel_klimenko; P114: GoodMood Photo; P114: Rixie; P116: raspirator; P116: digitalista; P116: SvetaZi; P116: georgepontinojr; P116: rolffimages; P116: raspirator; P116: Khakimullin; P121_125: Piotr Urakau; P121_125: Kapitosh; P126_127: designec; P128_131: YummyBuum; P130: totallyout. Synonyms and pronuciation from www.thesaurus.com.

The publisher has made every effort to trace and contact all copyright holders before publication. If notified, the publisher will rectify any errors or omissions as early as possible.

Welcome Teachers

to the Star Character Series, a collection of student working portfolios dedicated to character and cognitive development!

Recommended for AGES 8-12

EQ + IQ = :)

We believe that the education of emotional intelligence such as teamwork and communication is just as important as the traditional education of academics such as typing and math proficiency.

What does it look like to be a courageous digital citizen, feel like to be a courageous athlete, or sound like to be a courageous musician?

Wider Accessibility, Better Differentiation

Each page spread offers 2 unique learning opportunities under the same sub-strand: the left page is a widely-approachable experience, while the right page offers a more demanding challenge!

Experience Courage
in multiple contexts

- **7** major subject areas
- **32** sub-strands
- **9** multiple intelligences
- **10** reflection opportunities

Designed in consideration of the scope and sequences of the International Baccalaureate Organization and curricula from the US, UK, Canada and Australia.

Share your inspiration!

We encourage students to send us their stories about how they became even more courageous! Send us an email (p. 128), a pen pal letter (p. 129), or pages from your students' portfolios to share inspiration with other children around the world!

Welcome Students! You're in for some fun adventures on the following pages, but before you get on with it, I'd like to quickly share a few ideas with you!

You are ALREADY courageous!

Life requires courage from every person, every day. Whether it's making a decision or trying something new, each day presents challenges that we overcome with courage. You are already courageous, and so is everyone else.

You can become even more courageous!

Your attitude has a lot to do with your success and happiness.

Growth Mindset is a positive attitude which helps people learn and improve. If you have it **set** in your **mind** that you can **grow**, you can with practice and commitment!

This book has over 150 exercises for growing your courage!

You are THE BOSS of your Growth!

There will be times when your teacher assigns you a page in this book, but there will be other times when you get to pick too! Student agency means that you take charge of your own learning. You look at the choices, and you make the decisions!

Read through the Table of Constellations and choose 2 pages you'd like to try first! You can also use the Table of Constellations as a checklist of completion. Just tick off the star after you finish a page!

First Page I want to try
_____

Second Page I want to try
_____

After looking through the Table of Constellations and skimming through the book, write 2 goals for yourself that you would like to achieve while completing some or all of these activities. How do you want to grow as a courageous person?

GOAL #1 _____
_____

GOAL #2 _____
_____

Be the star you are and have fun becoming even more courageous!

TABLE OF CONSTELLATIONS

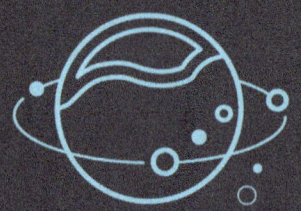

REFERENCES AND WARM-UPS... 11

Meaning and More .... 12 ★

Vital Statistics .... 13 ★

Quality Quotations .... 14 ★

Tons of Translations .... 15 ★

Searching for Synonyms .... 16 ★

Aligning the Antonyms .... 17 ★

Logo Mojo .... 18 ★

Awesome Analogies .... 19 ★

Reflection .... 20 ★

LANGUAGE... 21

Flash Fiction *(Writing)* .... 22 ★

Six-Pack Exercise *(Writing)* .... 23 ★

Post it! *(Reading)* .... 24 ★

Character vs. Conflict *(Reading)* .... 25 ★

Hear Me Out *(Speaking and Listening)* .... 26 ★

Over the Rainbow *(Speaking and Listening)* .... 27 ★

Video Game Review *(Media Literacy)* .... 28 ★

Hurry Up! *(Media Literacy)* .... 29 ★

Reflection .... 30 ★

MATHEMATICS... 31

Ghost of a Chance *(Data Handling and Probability)* .... 32 ★

Big Kid Questions *(Data Handling and Probability)* .... 33 ★

The Width of Worry *(Measurement)* .... 34 ★

Extreme Couraging *(Measurement)* .... 35 ★

~~Scary~~ Silly Shapes *(Geometry)* .... 36 ★

Treasure Map Challenge *(Geometry)* .... 37 ★

Breaking the Habit *(Pattern and Algebra)* .... 38 ★

Chop Chop! *(Pattern and Algebra)* .... 39 ★

Magnitude with Attitude *(Number)* .... 40 ★

Operation Hero *(Number)* .... 41 ★

Reflection .... 42 ★

ARTS... 43

Body Paint *(Visual Arts)* .... 44 ★

Mask Task *(Visual Arts)* .... 45 ★

The Beat of Bravery *(Music)* .... 46 ★

Historical Tunes *(Music)* .... 47 ★

Strike a Pose *(Dance and Movement)* .... 48 ★

A Bold Boogie *(Dance and Movement)* .... 49 ★

Puppet Power *(Drama)* .... 50 ★

Someone Else's Shoes *(Drama)* .... 51 ★

Show Those Photos *(Media Arts)* .... 52 ★

Moment of Truth *(Media Arts)* .... 53 ★

Reflection .... 54 ★

SCIENCE... 55

Creepy Critters *(Life)*
56 ★

Spooky Stages *(Life)*
57 ★

Inventive Risk-takers *(Energy)*
58 ★

"Paranormal" Forces *(Energy)*
59 ★

Scary Stuff *(Matter)*
60 ★

Properties of Prowess *(Matter)*
61 ★

Alien Theory *(Earth and Space)*
62 ★

Freaky Phenomena *(Earth and Space)*
63 ★

Reflection
64 ★

PERSONAL, SOCIAL, AND PHYSICAL HEALTH... 65

I'm Good *(Personal Well-being and Identity)*
66 ★

Meanie Mistakes *(Personal Well-being and Identity)*
67 ★

Mark Your Calendar *(Interactions and Relationships)*
68 ★

Bully Boycott *(Interactions and Relationships)*
69 ★

Straighten Out Stereotypes *(Intercultural Awareness)*
70 ★

Courage in Common *(Intercultural Awareness)*
71 ★

Tastebud Teasers *(Active Living and Nutrition)*
72 ★

Motivate Your Motors *(Active Living and Nutrition)*
73 ★

Reflection
74 ★

HUMANITIES AND SOCIAL STUDIES... 75

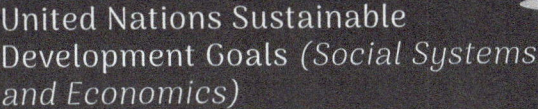

United Nations Sustainable Development Goals *(Social Systems and Economics)* .... 76 ★

Quality Education *(Social Systems and Economics)* .... 77 ★

Matchmaking *(Societal Structure and Culture)* .... 78 ★

Nice to Meet You *(Societal Structure and Culture)* .... 79 ★

A Series of Fortunate Events *(Time, Continuity, and Change)* .... 80 ★

Tearing Down Walls *(Time, Continuity, and Change)* .... 81 ★

Map of My Town *(Civilizations and Natural Environments)* .... 82 ★

Heroes of My Town *(Civilizations and Natural Environments)* .... 83 ★

Why the Waste? *(Resources and the Natural World)* .... 84 ★

Paper, ~~Rock~~ Markers, ~~Scissors~~ Tape *(Resources and the Natural World)* .... 85 ★

Ecuador *(Geography and Global Connections)* .... 86 ★

Fairtrade Bananas *(Geography and Global Connections)* .... 87 ★

Reflection .... 88 ★

TECHNOLOGY... 89

Household Heroes *(Hardware and Appliances)* .... 90 ★

Grasping New Gadgets *(Hardware and Appliances)* .... 91 ★

Pesky Programs *(Software and Applications)* .... 92 ★

Valiant Video *(Software and Applications)* .... 93 ★

Clickbait *(Internet)* .... 94 ★

Keywords and Phrases *(Internet)* .... 95 ★

Report Cyberbullying! *(Digital Citizenship)* .... 96 ★

Fair Use vs. Copyright *(Digital Citizenship)* .... 97 ★

Reflection .... 98 ★

MULTIPLE INTELLIGENCES... 99

Verbal-linguistic 100 ★

Mathematical-logical 102 ★

Visual-spatial 104 ★

Musical 106 ★

Bodily-kinesthetic 108 ★

Intrapersonal 110 ★

Interpersonal 112 ★

Naturalist 114 ★

Existential 116 ★

Reflection 118 ★

REFLECTIONS AND WRAP-UPS... 119

Congratulations! 120 ★

Doodle Diary 121 ★

Grand Reflection 126 ★

Email to the Stars 128 ★

Letter to the Stars 129 ★

Join the fun! 130 ★

Meet the Entire Constellation! 131 ★

References and Warm-Ups

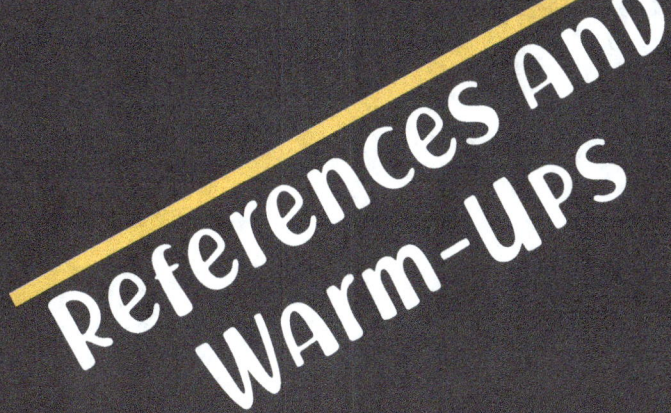

1. Meaning and More
root, Latin, suffix, definition

2. Vital Statistics
syllables, consonants, morphemes, typography

3. Quality Quotations
meaning, words of wisdom, inspiration, J.K. Rowling

4. Tons of Translations
languages, conversion, gender, pronunciation

5. Searching for Synonyms
word search, spelling, detail, diagonal

6. Aligning the Antonyms
crossword puzzle, vertical, horizontal, crisscross

7. Logo Mojo
words, images, messages, design

8. Awesome Analogies
comparison, connection, alike, symbolism

Courageous

Meaning and More

Definition:
Likely to take action from the heart, not stopped by fear

coura

cour: (root) from Latin cor, meaning heart

age: (suffix) adding an element of action

Part of Speech: Adjective
Origin: France
Pronunciation: KUH - rey - juhs
Age: over 703 years old

Vital Statistics

Letters: 10

Vowels: 6

Consonants: 4   Stems: 4

Ascenders: 0   Counters: 13   Eyes: 1

Descenders: 1   Apertures: 7   Ears: 1

Syllables: 3   Double Stories: 4   Shoulders: 0

geous

ous: (suffix) making a noun an adjective

Morphemes: 3

Roots: 1   Bowls: 1   Spines: 1

Affixes: 2   Cross Bars: 1   Arms: 1

Prefixes: 0   Cross Strokes: 0   Legs: 0

Suffixes: 2   Vertices: 0   Feet: 3

Joints: 4

13 Courageous

QUALITY QUOTATIONS

"It takes courage to grow up and become who you really are."

E.E. Cummings

Mark Twain

"Courage is resistance to fear, mastery of fear — not absence of fear."

"The most courageous act is still to think for yourself. Aloud."

Coco Chanel

Maya Angelou

"Courage is the most important of all the virtues because without courage, you can't practice any other virtue consistently."

"Scared is what you're feeling. Brave is what you're doing."

Emma Donoghue

J.K. Rowling

"It takes a great deal of bravery to stand up to our enemies, but just as much to stand up to our friends."

Whose quote is your favorite?

_____

What does it mean to you?

_____
_____
_____
_____
_____
_____

Now try to write your own famous quotation about courage!

_____
_____
_____
_____
_____

TONS OF TRANSLATIONS

COURAGEOUS

In addition to the ones on the right, there are so many other awesome languages out there! Research other world languages and find out what words they have for C O U R A G E O U S!

Language: _____
Courageous Translation:
_____

Language: _____
Courageous Translation:
_____

Language: _____
Courageous Translation:
_____

Language: _____
Courageous Translation:
_____

Language: _____
Courageous Translation:
_____

mutig
German

kulimba mtima
Chichewa

valiente
Spanish

ujasiri
Swahili

courageux (masculine)
French

corajosa (feminine)
Portuguese

moedig
Dutch

hrabar
Croatian

ua siab loj
Hmong

pogumen
Slovenian

moedige
Afrikaans

ushingi
Shona

koa
Hawaiian

cesur
Turkish

hrabar
Croatian

curajos
Romanian

lototele
Samoan

isibindi
Zulu

modig
Norwegian

matapang
Filipino

Courageous

SEARCHING FOR SYNONYMS

```
A O T S T R O N G B C D S Q W R S D G C
X D V B N M K J H G N B V C X Z A A W E
D F V U K P L Q E T U L O S E R L R W S
D C F E A D V E N T U B O U S A A I T V
A G H G N U N V X Z E W P I N R J N K L
F R G T Y T V C D V S A E T Z I O G N J
L N N N H R U F A E L P O N J N H B V E
K E O P I K N R Y C Z X S D E G F C A Q
W R S D V G D H O J U K M J H O L P U Y
T V L V C D A S T U Y Y B T H G Y B N I
K Y I H B R U F V E S D E W S X F V A N
I J O O L P N Y G T T F S A Z X A S F S
R B N H E R T I C J U H Y T G E V A R B
V C H X P I E N G Y G Q C Y I O P M A B
H Y E C Z X D E M Y B G H T F R D C I D
E F A T V B O L P J O U H G Y T B C D F
R D R S A Q W X C V L N H G T Y U J I N
O V T X Z A S A W D D R F T G Y H U H J
I S E O M E N O M E N O J M I K J N B G
C F D D R F G R I T T Y S S E L R A E F
```

WORD BANK

adventurous	brave	bold
gutsy	heroic	resolute
daring	strong	gritty
fearless	nervy	unafraid
lionhearted	undaunted	galant

ALIGNING THE ANTONYMS

WORD BANK

afraid	yielding	mild
meek	shy	timid
faint-hearted	fearful	cowardly
irresolute	unadventurous	delicate
gentle	weak	cautious

17 Courageous

LOGO MOJO

Graphic design is a fun form of art that combines pictures or designs with writing. A common example of graphic design is a logo. Have a look at some of the examples on this page, as well as the Star Character Series logo on the cover of this book. Combine the word courage, courageous, or one of the synonyms from page 16 with artwork to create an official logo for being a risk-taker!

18 References and Warm-Ups

Awesome Analogies

ANIMAL
COLOR FRUIT
TREE
WEATHER NUMBER
TOOL
SHAPE SONG CLOTHING
GAME FOOD SMELL
HOLIDAY MUSICAL INSTRUMENT
JEWELRY DRINK
FAMOUS PERSON
SEA CREATURE TOY SOUND
BIRD DESSERT
STATE OF MATTER ART

IF COURAGE WERE...

A FORM OF TRANSPORTATION, it would be a rocket because it can send people to the stars!

A PIECE OF FURNITURE, it would be a rocking chair because even though it swings you back and forth sometimes, you can trust that you're stable.

Choose ideas from the star above and come up with some of your own analogies!

If courage were _____, it would be _____ because _____.

If courage were _____, it would be _____ because _____.

If courage were _____, it would be _____ because _____.

References and Warm-Ups Reflection

1. What are some new things you learned about the meaning of courage?

2. Based on the quality of your work in this chapter, what is one goal you have for working in other chapters?

3. What other activity could you design for this chapter?

LANGUAGE

1 Writing
word choice, story, punctuation, editing

2 Reading
fluency, vocabulary, characters, conflicts

3 Speaking and Listening
tone of voice, perspective, active hearing, attention

4 Media Literacy
video games, realism, persuasive techniques, advertisements

FLASH FICTION

Write a flash fiction piece (a super short story) about you confronting one of your fears. How will you gather the courage to face it, and what will happen when you do?

_____
(TITLE)

Six-Pack Exercise

Follow these steps to see how much editing can improve your writing!

1.

Step 1: Write a paragraph that includes at least 3 sentences about the following:
- your own definition of "courageous"
- an example of what it looks like
- one way to become even more couragous.

2.

Step 2: Rewrite your paragraph using at least 7 fewer words.

3.

Step 3: Change at least 5 words with a thesaurus and rewrite your paragraph.

4.

Step 4: Choose a partner to read your paragraph for spelling, punctuation, and word choice. Your partner should write 1 compliment and 2 suggestions in Box 4.

5.

Step 5: Rewrite your paragraph using your partner's suggestions (if you believe they will improve your paragraph).

6.

Step 6: Reflect on how your paragraph has changed. Is it better? Why or why not? What other steps can you create to improve a piece of writing?

23 | Courageous

POST IT!

Look around your classroom at everything there is to read - posters, signs, book covers.... Write your name on 3 post-its and then walk around the room, sticking them on any poster, display, or word you can't read. Write the words you couldn't read in the post-its below and try new ways to figure out how to read these words. It may be asking a friend, sounding them out, or working with a teacher. Explain how you figured out how to read each word by trying something new.

Character Vs. Conflict

Every story has conflict that characters need to solve by taking risks. Choose 2 books you've read and write down the title, a character's name, and courageous acts that character performed in the story.

Title: _____
Character: _____
Acts of Courage: _____
_____
_____
_____

Title: _____
Character: _____
Acts of Courage: _____
_____
_____
_____

Choose a new book to read and pay careful attention to how characters use courage to overcome their conflicts. Draw the cover of your book below and record the pages you read in the chart. After you finish the book, describe how one of the charcters showed courage.

Date	Pages Read	Date	Pages Read

Courageous

Hear Me Out

Review the 3 statements below and decide whether you agree or disagree with each one. Be sure to determine reasons why you've made your decisions. Then talk to your classmates and find someone for each topic whose opinion is different than yours. Share your perspectives and listen carefully to one another in order to truly understand both points of view. You don't need to change your mind after your discussion, but find good points that your partners make for their opinions, and write them below.

> Although it is important to be courageous, there are also moments when it's better not to be courageous.

Agree   Disagree

> Some people are just born more courageous than others. That's the way they are and won't ever really change that much.

Agree   Disagree

> Trying too many new things makes people spread themselves out too thin, so they never get very good at any one thing.

Agree   Disagree

My Partners' Thoughts

Good points about my partner's opinion:

_____
_____
_____
_____
_____
_____
_____
_____
_____

Good points about my partner's opinion:

_____
_____
_____
_____
_____
_____
_____
_____
_____

Good points about my partner's opinion:

_____
_____
_____
_____
_____
_____
_____
_____
_____

Language: Speaking and Listening

OVER THE RAINBOW

The structure of many stories goes up and then down like a rainbow. It begins with a setting, establishing time, place and characters, and then rises with an action that prevents characters from being happy. The climax occurs at the highest point of the story, where the main problem is now somehow possible to solve. The story slides down toward the end as solutions fall into place. Everything is wrapped up in the end at the bottom, where the problems are solved and a lesson is learned, or a theme is left to consider. With a partner, take turns telling each other a story about a courageous character who solves a problem. As you listen, fill in the elements of the rainbow below, and then compare notes to check how accurately you spoke and listened.

Video Game Review

Do you play video games? If you do, you might have noticed that the point of the game is to overcome some sort of obstacle. Though the characters and challenges may be different, a challenge of any kind requires traits like commitment, stamina and courage. Reflect on a video game you play and answer the questions on this page.

What is the name of your video game?
_____

Which character do you play in the game?
_____

What does your character look like? _____
_____

What challenges does your character face?
_____
_____

How does your character overcome these challenges?
_____
_____

Do you and your character have anything in common?
_____
_____

Is your character courageous? Why / why not?
_____
_____
_____

Are your character's problems realistic?
_____

Are the ways in which your character solves problems realistic? _____
_____

Do you feel video games give people good opportunities to learn how to become more courageous? Why?
_____
_____
_____
_____
_____

Hurry Up!

Advertisers use persuasive techniques to convince customers to purchase something, and sometimes these techniques put pressure on people. Some of these strategies include the four Greek words below:

Pathos
Greek for **suffering** or **experience**, this strategy attempts to pull on the heartstrings of customers by making them feel emotional about the product or service.

Ethos
Greek for **character**, this strategy gives credibility to a person or larger community who endorses the product or service.

Logos
Greek for **word**, **opinion**, or **reason**, this strategy explains facts, statistics and other logical reasons why the customer should buy the product or service.

Kairos
Greek for **opportune moment**, this strategy gives customers a sense of urgency by explaining that now is the perfect time to buy the product or service.

Find an advertisement that intimidates or "bullies" someone into buying the product. Draw or paste it below and provide advice to customers for how to be brave and not fall for intimidating advertising.

PLACE AD BELOW BEFORE IT'S TOO LATE!

What persuasive technique is used in this ad? What advice would you give to someone who might feel pressured to buy this product?

_____
_____
_____
_____
_____
_____
_____
_____
_____

Courageous

Language Reflection

1. What was your favorite activity? Why did you like it more than the other pages?

2. If you had to complete this chapter again, what would you do differently?

3. What do you think your teacher would say about your work in this chapter?

MATHEMATICS

1 Data Handling and Probability
statistics, chances, tallies, bar graphs

2 Measurement
tools, size, units, amount

3 Geometry
shapes, angles, grids, maps

4 Pattern and Algebra
repetition, habits, fear rating, associative property

5 Number
magnitude, multiplication, operations, explanations

GHOST OF A CHANCE

Take some time to brainstorm all the things you worry might happen. Choose 4 of these worries and write them down in the 1st column in the table below. Did you have to deal with any of the things that worry you **today**? If so, make a tally in the Today column. Did it happen more than once today? If so, tally the number of times you were confronted with this concern. If you did not have to deal with this concern today, write a zero (0) in the Today column, and move on to the Yesterday column until you complete the row. Complete all rows by thinking about each worry. Did the concern happen yesterday? Last week? Last month? Last year? Tally this data for all 4 of your fears.

Worry	Today	Yesterday	Last Week	Last Month	Last Year

Now analyze your completed chart. What are the chances you will have to confront your concern?

Multiple tallies in most columns	Certain?
Some tallies in Today / Yesterday / Last Week columns	Likely?
A few tallies in Last Month / Last Year columns	Unlikely?
No tallies in any columns	Impossible?

If any of your concerns are certain to happen, what can you do to handle them?

_____

_____

If any of your concerns are unlikely or perhaps impossible to happen, they might not be worth worrying about at all! How can you let go of this concern?

_____

_____

BIG KID QUESTIONS

Are you ever shy around older students? Have you ever thought about why? Sometimes we're intimidated by things just because we don't know a lot about them. Write some questions you might ask older students that would teach you more about them and what it's like to be their age. Then create a graph of your findings. An example has been done for you below.

Example Question: What time do you go to bed on school nights?

8:00	𝍷𝍷𝍷𝍷𝍷 |||
9:00	𝍷𝍷𝍷𝍷𝍷	
10:00	|||
11:00		

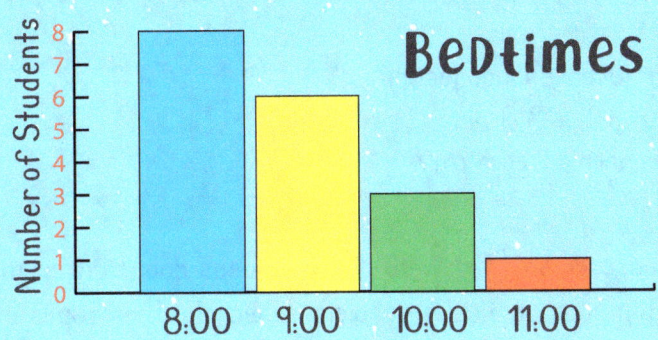

Use the space below to show your research. Write your question and create a tally chart. Then survey older students and record their answers in your chart. Finally, create a graph to represent your data.

THE WIDTH OF WORRY

How could you measure your fears to see how big they really are? List your top 4 fears and explore how you could measure them. Putting your fears into numerical measurements might help you deal with them.

Length of a juvenile Madagascar hissing cockroach = 3.8 cm
(That's smaller than a french fry!)

Angle of the bite of a saltwater crocodile = 46°
(A kitten yawns wider than that!)

Read the measurements below to give you ideas about different ways you could measure your fears. If these don't work for your particular problem, research other types of measurements, as there are many out there!

- length
- width
- perimeter
- area
- mass
- volume
- time duration
- temperature
- flow rate
- angle
- energy
- sound

Fear	Measurement with units	How I measured this fear

Have these numbers changed the way you look at your fears? How?

_____
_____
_____
_____

EXTREME COURAGING

Imagine a new sport has been admitted into the next Olympics. It's called Extreme Couraging. You are on the board of directors to determine how the most courageous participants will win. Choose 3 events that the risk-takers must compete in. Explain what they have to do, how they will be measured, and in which units they will be measured.

Event	Description of Activity	Measurement	Units

In the High Jump event, olympians must jump over a horizontal pole. Heights are measured in meters, centimeters and millimeters or feet and inches. The weights in weightlifting are measured in kilograms.

In addition to weight and height, numerous other measurements are taken in the Olympics, including speed, length, and distance. What units might these examples be measured in? What other examples can you think of for your events?

~~Scary~~ Silly Shapes

Think of some of the things you're afraid of. Spiders? Aliens? Monsters? All of these things are simply made up of shapes. Can you use some 2D shapes to create a fun picture of your fear? After you've finished, count up the number of corners and sides your fear has. Calculating some of these statistics might reduce something scary into a harmless pile of shapes!

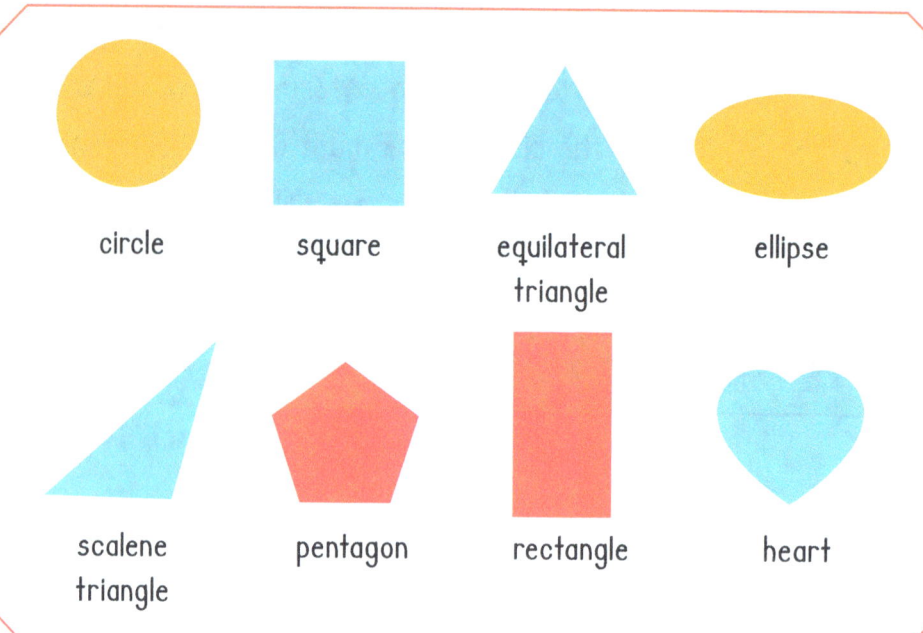

Total number of corners: _____

Total number of sides: _____

Which shapes did you use?

TREASURE MAP CHALLENGE

Make your way through this treasure map of perils by following the directions and answering the questions below. Be sure to come up with creative answers that exhibit signs of courage. Running away from something, for example, is not a creatively courageous solution.

Begin in the black square with the white X. Travel 9 squares east and 1 square south. What do you find there, and how would you show courage to handle this situation?

_____
_____

From that point travel 2 squares north and 2 squares east. What do you find there, and how would you show courage to handle this situation?

_____
_____

From that point travel 5 squares north, 9 squares west, and 1 square south. What do you find there, and how would you show courage to handle this situation?

_____
_____

From that point travel 3 squares west, 4 squares north, and 4 squares east. What do you find there, and how would you show courage to handle this situation?

_____
_____

Courageous

Breaking the Habit

We all have habits, which are actions that we repeat over and over again. Some habits are healthy, like brushing our teeth every night before bed or helping our family around the house, and some habits are unhealthy, like biting our nails or eating too much candy all the time.

Brainstorm a list of healthy and unhealthy habits you have. Then choose and circle one of your unhealthy habits to reflect on. Draw a picture, plan a timeline, create a chart or write a paragraph that shows how this behavior is a pattern.

Healthy Habits	Unhealthy Habits

Think hard about why you maintain this pattern. Why do you continue to repeat this behavior?

Patterns can be broken by consistently replacing the old behavior with something new. What action can you take and repeat until it turns into a new, healthier behavior that replaces the old, unhealthy one?

CHOP CHOP!

The associative property in mathematics lets you add numbers in different ways and still end up with the same sum. If you take a big number and chop it into pieces, the smaller numbers are more easily managed than the larger numbers. Try using the associative property with a fear of yours. Select something that worries you and give it a FEAR RATING from 10 - 100, 10 being no big deal, 100 being the end of the world. Chop the big number into 2 smaller numbers that add up to your original number. Assign each number a detail of your issue. Then chop each of these pieces into 2 smaller numbers. Assign each of these numbers another detail. Check out this example below.

Breaking down a fear lets you focus on specific factors that are easier to overcome. In the case above, you could plan for each of the 4 bottom details. If you start to stutter, cough a lot. If you think you might start to sweat, wear a couple layers so the sweat doesn't show through your shirt too soon. If your hands shake, bring a chair up to set your papers and rest your hands upon. To avoid standing in silence, practice your speech so many times you can say it in your sleep. By preparing for these details, you'll be ready to handle your concerns if they come up. Now chop up one of your own fears and write plans beneath each detail that will help you avoid them.

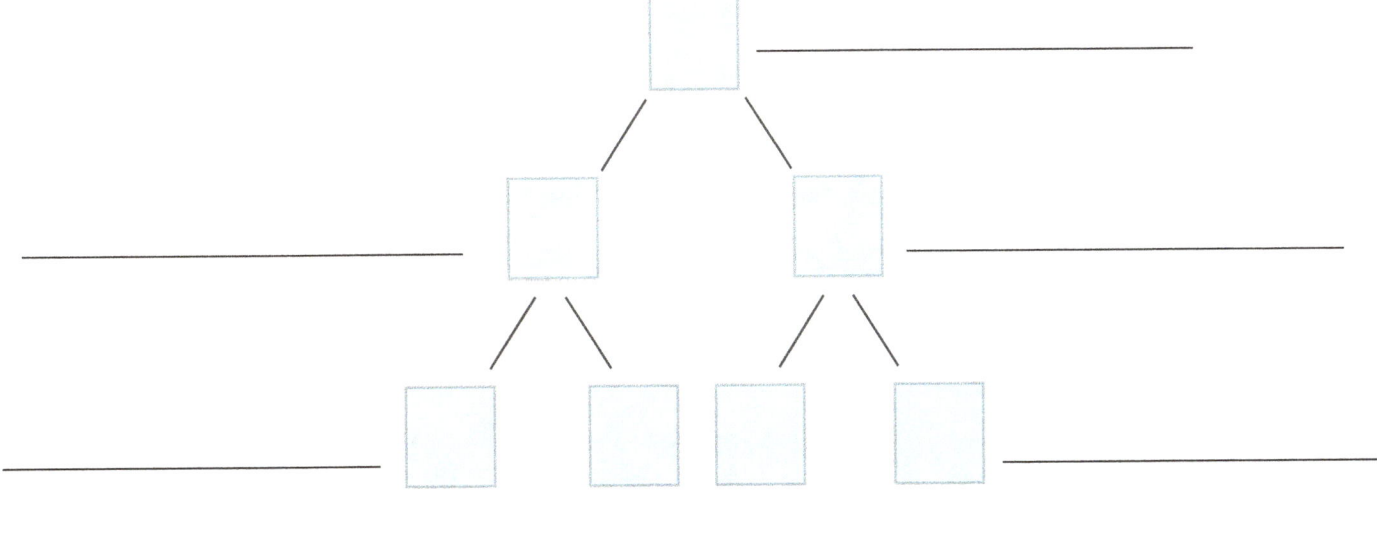

Magnitude with Attitude

The more often you do anything, the easier it can become because you get better at it. This includes calling upon your courage in intimidating situations. In the shapes below, draw pictures or write a story based on the captions. Include the math equations to see how the magnitude of fear and courage can divide and multiply. In the first part of the story, your courage level must be a multiple of 10.

Story Title: _____

40 Math: Number

Operation Hero

Think creatively about the following 4 operations and describe through metaphor or simile what you are really doing with numbers when you work with each operation. Be imaginative and clear in your explanations. Below is an example.

Addition: When adding, numbers are stacked on top of one another like a totem pole is stacked with animals. The sizes of the numbers are like the sizes of animals, so if you add small numbers, you get a short totem pole with a mouse and a sparrow stacked only so high. If you add larger numbers, you get a tall totem pole with 3 giraffes on top of one another.

ADDITION

_____
_____
_____
_____

SUBTRACTION

_____
_____
_____
_____

MULTIPLICATION

_____
_____
_____
_____

DIVISION

_____
_____
_____
_____

Which one of the 4 operations requires the most courage from mathematicians? Why?

_____
_____

If numbers were little people, which operation would require the most courage from them? Why?

_____
_____

Mathematics Reflection

1 What was your favorite activity? Why did you like it more than the other pages?

2 Which page are you least proud of? What do you think went wrong?

3 How would you describe what it means to be a courageous mathematician?

ARTS

1 Visual Arts
symbolism, decoration, materials, masks

2 Music
beat, instruments, rhythm, repetition

3 Dance and Movement
position, body, form, choreography,

4 Drama
puppets, characters, role play, perspective

5 Media Arts
photography, shape, video, effects

Body Paint

The people of the ancient Aztec, Inca, and Mayan cultures would sometimes decorate themselves in body paint before special ceremonies and battles. The eagle warrior was a particular symbol of courage.

Why do you think this symbol showed courage?

_____
_____
_____
_____

Following the style of this eagle warrior, design your own symbol that you could paint on your body before your next confrontation with fear. What image would give you strength?

Mask Task

Masks have been created and worn for centuries across cultures all over the world. Which mask below would you wear to a Ceremony of Courage? Why?

Design a mask in the space below to be worn by someone who is afraid to do something. Bring your mask to life by creating it with a paper plate and other art supplies!

THE BEAT OF BRAVERY

The beat of music has been called the heartbeat of a song. Choose a song you like that has a beat to it that makes you feel strong, courageous and motivated to do something positive for yourself or others. Describe how the beat can create this mood.

Song title: _____

How the beat creates the mood: _____
_____

Close your eyes and imagine how your heart beats from the moment you know you need to be brave until the moment after your courageous act is over. What journey does your heart take? Experiment with different instruments and compose a short piece that represents the musical crescendo of courage. Describe below how you used 3 instruments in different ways. Then put them together and record your song to play for your family and friends!

Song title: _____

Instrument 1: _____ Describe your beat on the lines below using words or notes.

Instrument 2: _____ Describe your beat on the lines below using words or notes.

Instrument 3: _____ Describe your beat on the lines below using words or notes.

HISTORICAL TUNES

Music has been enjoyed by people and communities for thousands of years, serving hundreds of purposes.

What purpose does music serve in your life?

_____
_____
_____
_____

Research the role music played in a past society and choose one culture that used music specifically for conjuring up courage before particularly stressful moments, such as war, sickness, or coming of age. Describe how some of the musical concepts below were used for this purpose.

Instruments ♪

_____
_____
_____
_____
_____

Rhythm ♪

_____
_____
_____
_____
_____

Harmony ♪

_____
_____
_____
_____
_____

Repetition ♩

_____
_____
_____
_____
_____

47 Courageous

STRIKE A POSE

Study the different people on this page and circle the risk-taker you feel is showing the most courage through dance. Explain why you chose your selection.

_____
_____
_____
_____
_____
_____
_____

Can you imitate the positions above? Create some of your own moves that capture courage in a single position. Describe your pose, illustrate your pose, or glue a photo of yourself below.

Arts: Dance

A BOLD BOOGIE

Analyze these dance forms and explain how they could represent a Dance of Courage.

Now get up and dance! Choreograph your own Dance of Courage and use the space below to describe it and explain how it tells a story of courage. Include illustrations and photographs as well!

49 Courageous

Puppet Power

Think about a puppet show you've seen. How did the characters and story reflect problems of people in real life? If you've never seen a puppet show, think of a cartoon you've seen, as puppet shows are sort of like live cartoons.

_____
_____
_____

Perform your own puppet show in which a puppet solves a problem with courage. First use the space below to sketch some ideas for your puppet designs and then brainstorm what will happen in your story.

Puppet Designs	**Story Ideas**

Someone Else's Shoes

You may have heard of the popular phrase that claims you can't truly understand someone unless you walk around in their shoes. Doing this requires you to role-play and pretend you are someone else. How does role-playing help you understand someone better?

_____
_____
_____
_____
_____

With 2 partners, choose a typical situation in the lives of kids your age where courage is required. It might involve bullies, friends, teachers, family members, school work, sports.... Create a scene with 3 characters and reenact the situation 3 times so each of you has the opportunity to play the role of every character. Then reflect on how playing the different roles helped you better understand the courage represented in this skit.

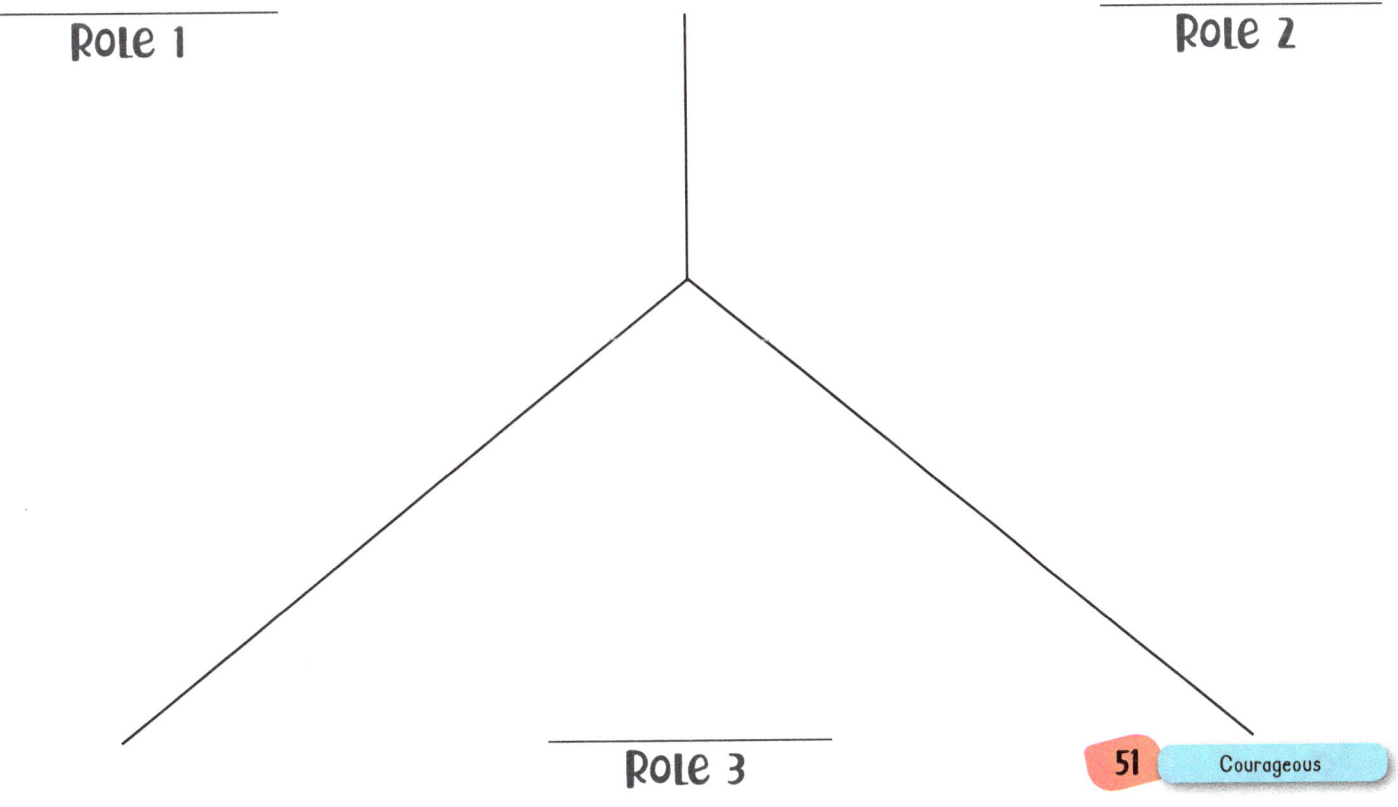

Show Those Photos

Study this photograph and explain how some of the elements of photography are used to create a sense of courage in the scene.

Take your own photos that include elements of photography that create a courageous mood or effect. Explain how you used some of these elements below, and post one of your photos in the box on the right.

_____
_____
_____
_____
_____

Elements of Photography

LINE (paths): _____
_____

FORM (3D objects): _____
_____

TEXTURE (details on forms): _____
_____

PATTERN (repetition of elements): _____
_____

COLOR (warm, cool, primary, etc.): ____
_____

SPACE (distance between elements): ___
_____

Moment of Truth

Find a moment in a movie when a character shows courage and describe how some of the elements of video in the box to the left help to create the courageous mood in the scene.

- SOUND EFFECTS
- MUSIC
- LIGHTING
- CAMERA ANGLE
- CLIP DURATION
- SUBJECT
- SCENERY
- DIALOGUE

Movie title: _____

Moment of truth: _____

Some elements and how they create a mood of courage: _____
_____

Record your own moment of truth or brief scene where a character shows courage in a situation. Describe your scene below and explain how you used some of the elements of video to enhance the courageous effect.

Scene description: _____
_____
_____
_____

Elements manipulated to create a courageous mood: _____
_____
_____

Courageous

Arts Reflection

1. What might other students think about your courage if they looked at your work in this chapter?

2. What was one positive experience you had when completing these activities?

3. How would you rate the pages in this chapter from 1 (fun) to 10 (boring)? Why?

SCIENCE

1 Life
animals, forms, butterflies, life stages

2 Energy
inventions, work, natural forces, ghosts

3 Matter
dentists, materials, properties, absorbancy

4 Earth and Space
aliens, elements, phenomena, fire rainbows

Courageous

CREEPY CRITTERS

Think about all the life forms on the planet, from bacteria and bed bugs to pigeons and piranhas. Choose 2 animals that make you nervous, queasy, or downright terrified and gather some information about them. Include a sketch or colorful illustration.

Animal: _____

	Body Shape (how it looks)	Locomotion (how it moves)	Vocals (how it sounds)	Texture (how it feels)

Animal: _____

	Body Shape (how it looks)	Locomotion (how it moves)	Vocals (how it sounds)	Texture (how it feels)

Do these animals have anything in common? Do they share certain characteristics, such as having sharp teeth, scaly skin, multiple legs, or no legs at all? Is it really the animal that bothers you, or something else?

_____

_____

_____

56 Science: Life

Spooky Stages

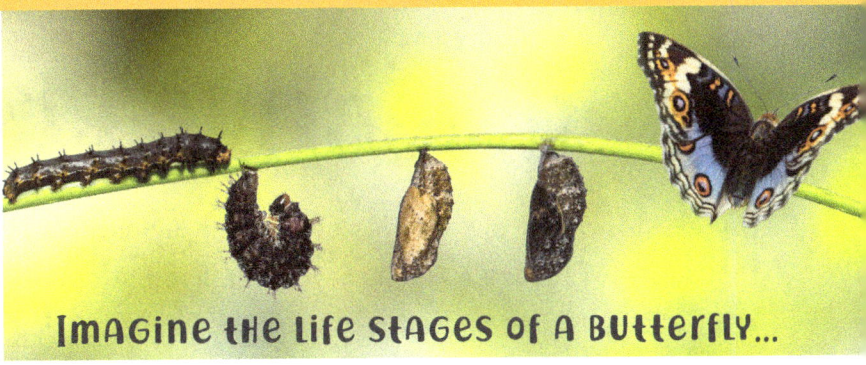

Imagine the life stages of a butterfly...

It begins inside a dark, confining egg that it needs to break out of. It crawls into the world as a tiny caterpillar small enough to be eaten by almost every other animal around. It furiously munches on leaves, hoping not to be eaten. It then begins to release silk from its head that it weaves with its mouth into a tight cocoon around its whole body. It remains trapped inside, like being zipped up in a sleeping bag... for days or even weeks! It finally emerges to discover that some of its legs are gone, two big wings stick out of its back, and its skin is a different color. It can no longer walk like an accordion but has to learn how to fly by jumping off a branch hundreds of times its own height....

Talk about some spooky stages!

Human life stages can sometimes be scary too. We grow through multiple stages that present different challenges. Circle one person above who you think is in a hard stage. Then answer the questions below.

What might happen during this life stage that you think will be hard to deal with?
_____
_____

What are some strategies people can use to be courageous when dealing with these problems?
_____
_____

If you've already been through this stage, how courageous were you when dealing with the struggles? If you have yet to enter this stage, how can you prepare to enter this life stage with courage?
_____
_____

Inventive Risk-Takers

Our world wasn't always this convenient. Inventions over thousands of years have improved our lives in countless ways. Many of these inventions do work for us, saving us energy for other activities. From the fundamental simple machines like the pulley, lever, and inclined plane to more complex inventions such as elevators, egg beaters, and drills, all of these were created by someone who worked hard to save the rest of us energy. During the design process they didn't know if their inventions would work, so it took courage and commitment to continue. Choose an invention that saves you energy in some way and research its inventor. Which obstacles did this courageous inventor overcome?

Image of your inventor or invention

Inventor: _____

Date and place of birth: _____

Invention: _____

Date and place of creation: _____

Main purpose of invention: _____

The story of courage: _____
_____
_____
_____
_____
_____
_____
_____

"Paranormal" Forces

Many ghost stories and other scary, "paranormal" phenomena have been explained through the universe's forces and energy. Research and learn about some of the examples below.

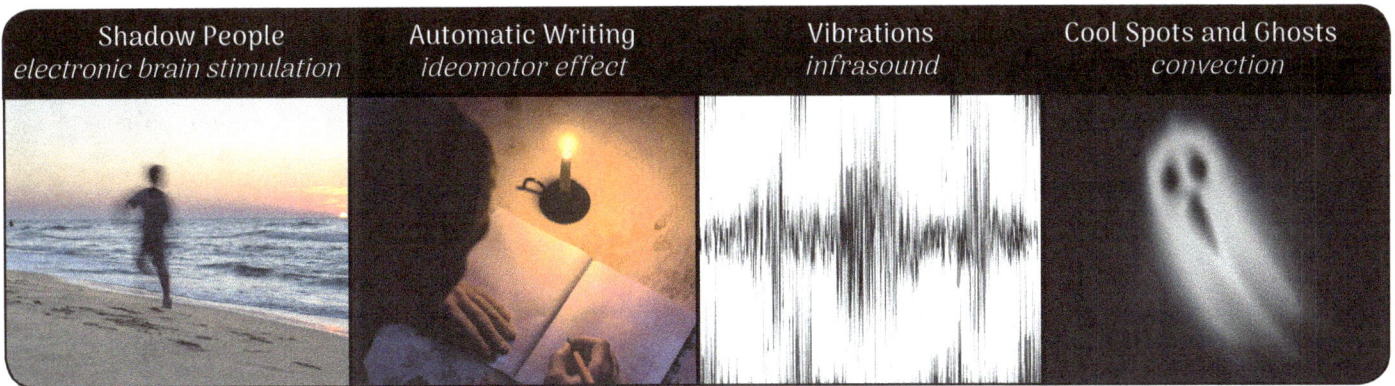

Shadow People — *electronic brain stimulation*
Automatic Writing — *ideomotor effect*
Vibrations — *infrasound*
Cool Spots and Ghosts — *convection*

Have you ever witnessed something spooky? Determine whether one of the forms of energy below might be responsible for your mystery. Draw a diagram or write a theory that links your mystery to either one of these forms of energy or another form of energy you might learn about.

Potential Energy (stored)	Kinetic Energy (motion)
• chemical • mechanical • nuclear • gravitational	• radiant • thermal • sound • electrical

SCARY STUFF

Sometimes just knowing what something is really made out of makes it less scary, like seeing the actor behind the mask of a monster in a movie. Have a look below at some of the components of a dentist (one of the top fears, although they're nothing to be afraid of).

Surgical masks are often made of polypropylene fabric, a chemical compound also used in water bottles and sunglasses.

Medical gloves include latex (a milky substance from plants) and nitrile rubber (a combination of acrylonitrile, a stinky liquid, and butadiene, an invisible gas).

Eyebrows are made of a protein called keratin, related to fingernails and deer antlers.

Dental mirrors include stainless steel (made of chemical elements like iron, carbon, and chromium), heated aluminum, and glass.

The uniform, often called scrubs for being used in a clean, "scrubbed" workplace, is made of polyester, a mix of air, water, coal and petroleum.

Some of the top fears kids have include closets, the space under the bed, scary animals from page 56, roller coasters, ghosts, aliens, insects, storms, bullies, elevators, vomiting, school presentations, mean teachers, tests, and pimples. Are you afraid of any of these? Choose one fear and investigate the "stuff" it's made of. Create a diagram of your fear below, labeling its various materials.

Properties of Prowess

Research the following properties of materials and write a brief definition for each one. Then imagine that prowess (another word for courage) were a tangible (touchable) material. Assign each of these properties of prowess a Courage Level number between 1 and 10, 1 being very low, and 10 being very high, and explain why. For example, would courage have high magnetism (8 or 9) or low magnetism (2 or 3)? Why?

Property	Definition	Courage Level	Why?
flexibility			
magnetism			
density			
transparency			
absorbancy			
mass			
volume			
conductivity			
strength			
solubility			

61 Courageous

ALIEN THEORY

Many people claim to have seen an unidentified flying object (UFO), and others even claim to have been abducted by aliens!

Here on earth there are specific elements that sustain life, including air, water, a source of food, and shelter from weather and extreme temperature. Are these elements also in space to support alien life? Are there different elements in space that could support life? Explore these questions and write an explanation that might reduce fear in those who believe they might be abducted by aliens one day.

Alien Explanation

_____
_____
_____
_____
_____
_____
_____
_____
_____
_____
_____
_____
_____

FREAKY PHENOMENA

Aurora Borealis

Sailing stones of Death Valley

The earth is host to many apparently mysterious phenomena. Pictured on this page are just a couple of them which have intimidated cultures across the world. Research one of the world's many phenomena and provide a brief scientific explanation for why there's nothing to be afraid of.

Other phenomena include:

- unrelated worldwide reports of similar sea monsters
- green flashes
- fire rainbows
- Bigfoot, Skunk Ape, or Yeren
- bioluminescence
- red tide
- the Bermuda Triangle
- Namibia's fairy circles

What other natural mysteries can you find?

There is no reason to fear _____ because

_____
_____
_____
_____
_____
_____
_____

My Source: _____

Science Reflection

1 How have you become a more courageous scientist?

2 What was your greatest strength when engaging with this chapter?

3 What was your greatest weakness when engaging with this chapter?

Personal, Social, and Physical Health

1. **Personal Well-being and Identity**
   self-worth, compliments, values, behavior

2. **Interactions and Relationships**
   old friends, new friends, bullies, responsibility

3. **Intercultural Awareness**
   culture, stereotypes, legends, similarities

4. **Active Living and Nutrition**
   tastebuds, new foods, motor skills, activities

I'm Good

The truth is, you really ARE special and unique. Maybe your parents told you that already, maybe your teachers too. But they (and this book) can tell you that a thousand times, and it won't really matter unless YOU recognize it for yourself.

Make a list, draw a picture, paste a collage or design a word splash of at least 20 things that are good about you. If you can't come up with at least 20 things, perhaps you're afraid to admit it? You're not being asked to brag, you're being asked to give yourself credit and appreciate the goodness within you.

Meanie Mistakes

We're all human, and we all make mistakes. It's hard to be nice to everyone all the time. We can always try to improve and learn from our mistakes though. True reflection of our mistakes takes courage and honesty. Think back to the last time you were mean to someone, laughed at someone, didn't let someone play with you, told a secret about someone, or somehow hurt someone's feelings. Replay this moment in your head a few times, from beginning to end, and then answer the questions below.

1. How did you benefit from this behavior, in this moment? How did it do something good for you?
_____
_____

2. Which of your values or beliefs did this behavior represent? Did it conflict with any of your values?
_____
_____

3. Was your behavior influenced by something or someone else? If so, how?
_____
_____

4. Why do you think you really did this? Were you really being... you?
_____
_____

5. What is one thing you will do to avoid repeating this behavior?
_____
_____

Mark Your Calendar

Making friends starts with getting to know people first. In the table below, make lists of all the kids in your class who you played with last week, and all the kids you haven't played with in a while.

Kids I played with last week	Kids I haven't played with lately... or ever

Your challenge next week is to spend each break period with one of the kids from this column. Choose a new person every time. Schedule your playtimes with these classmates in the calendar below. Draw extra rows for the number of breaks you have per day.

Monday	Tuesday	Wednesday	Thursday	Friday

After the week of playing with new people is over, reflect on your interactions. What was it like to play with all these different people? Did you make any new friends? Will you play with any of them again?

_____
_____
_____
_____

PSPH: Interactions and Relationships

Bully Boycott

Have you ever seen something like this happen on the playground?

Have you ever been this person?

Or this person?

Or this person?

Unfortunately people aren't always nice to each other, and mean people can sometimes be scary. It is your right to feel comfortable wherever you are, be it at home, on a playground, or at school. When someone bullies you, it is important to stand up to that person. Chat with some friends and come up with 2 things you could say to someone who is bullying you or someone else.

1. _____

2. _____

And now the hard part – standing up to the next bully you see. Any time you see someone being mean to someone else, tell that person that this treatment is unacceptable using the clever lines you came up with above. Use the table below to keep track of your courageous interactions and reflect on them.

What did the bully do?	What did you do or say?	How nervous were you?	How did the bully react?
		😊 🙂 😐 😟 😠	
		😊 🙂 😐 😟 😠	
		😊 🙂 😐 😟 😠	

Did your nervous rating get greener? Did it become easier to stand up to bullies with more practice?

_____

69 Courageous

STRAIGHTEN OUT STEREOTYPES

Choose 2 children you know whose cultures or home countries are different than yours. Write one of their names in each of the ovals below. Then brainstorm everything you think you know about that child's culture or country and write your thoughts down around the circle. See the list below for topic ideas.

- clothing
- food
- festivals
- communication styles
- games
- music
- dances
- ideas of what's beautiful
- ideas of what's ugly
- values
- religious beliefs
- government
- holidays
- famous people
- biases
- landscape
- nature
- family and gender roles
- jobs
- arts and crafts
- body language

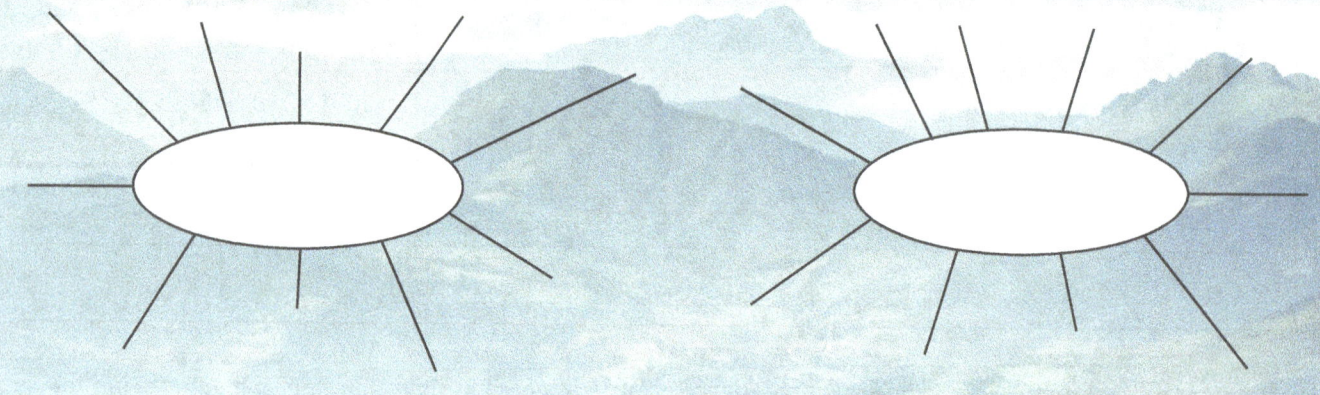

Might any of your ideas above be stereotypes of these cultures? Speak with the 2 children from these cultures and find out if any of your thoughts are true. Remember to use polite and respectful communication skills when sharing your ideas. In the space below reflect on your conversation and write down what you learned.

_____
_____
_____
_____
_____
_____

PSPH: Intercultural Awareness

COURAGE IN COMMON

Research a fairytale or legend from another culture. Find one with a character who must overcome obstacles with courageous acts. Summarize the story in the box below.

_____
_____
_____
_____
_____
_____
_____
_____
_____

How is this story of courage different than stories from your culture?

_____
_____

How is it similar?

_____
_____

Do you think the similarities between these 2 cultures extend to all other cultures?

_____
_____
_____

Tastebud Teasers

Did you know that tastebuds can change their minds about which foods they like? It's true! (Well, tastebuds don't have minds, but they CAN change.) Choose 5 healthy foods that you refuse to eat. (Be a risk-taker and choose the healthiest foods, even if they taste the worst!) For 2 weeks, try each of these foods 4 times and then reflect below on the experience. Write the date you tried each food and circle your facial expression.

 Yum!   Meh.   Ew.  Bleh!

Food	First Try	Second Try	Third Try	Fourth Try
	Date:	Date:	Date:	Date:
	Date:	Date:	Date:	Date:
	Date:	Date:	Date:	Date:
	Date:	Date:	Date:	Date:
	Date:	Date:	Date:	Date:

Did your ratings improve for each food over time? Did you rate honestly?

_____

What do you think would happen if you continued this tastebud experiment for 3 months?

_____

Motivate Your Motors

Your body needs regular movement, including exercises in both gross and fine motor skills. Gross motor skills involve your whole body, arms, or legs, while fine motor skills involve your hands and fingers. From the lists below choose 1 gross motor and 1 fine motor activity that you would like to become better at. Spend 20 minutes practicing these activities 4 times each week for 2 weeks.

Gross Motor Activities
- sports
- martial arts
- dance
- running
- swimming
- yoga
- parkour

Fine Motor Activities
- handwriting
- using scissors
- playing piano
- tracing / drawing
- collaging
- sewing / weaving
- beading

Schedule these activities into your calendar. Write down the name of the activity and the time when you will practice it. For example, you might write YOGA 9:00 - 9:20 in the Saturday column. You should have 8 activities scheduled each week. After you complete the 2 weeks, answer the questions below.

Sunday	Monday	Tuesday	Wednesday	Thursday	Friday	Saturday

Did you enjoy either of the activities? Discuss what was good and bad about each one.
_____
_____
_____

If you had to do this experience again, which activities would you choose instead, and why?
_____
_____

Courageous

PSPH Reflection

1 How did you help others while engaging in these activities?

2 What are some new things you learned about yourself?

3 What was one negative experience you had when completing these activities?

Humanities and Social Studies

1 Social Systems and Economics
sustainability, goals, quality education, targets

2 Societal Structure and Culture
people, interactions, communication, identity

3 Time, Continuity, and Change
history, future, events, influence

4 Civilizations and Natural Environments
places, maps, features, development

5 Resources and the Natural World
packaging, conservation, limitation, distribution

6 Geography and Global Connections
climate, Ecuador, Fairtrade, bananas

Courageous

SUSTAINABLE DEVELOPMENT GOALS

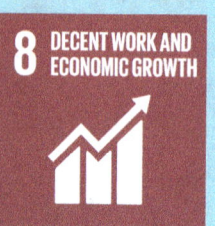

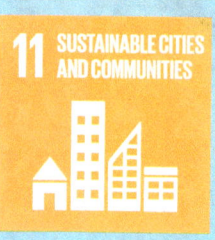

Visit the United Nations Sustainable Development Goals at

https://www.un.org/sustainabledevelopment/sustainable-development-goals/

Above are the 17 Sustainable Development Goals defined by the United Nations. After researching these goals on the website, answer the questions below.

Which goal do you feel will take the most courage to achieve? _____

Why do you think so? Refer to this goal's facts, figures and targets when explaining your answer.

_____
_____

How would you show courage to support this goal? What advice would you give to others?

_____
_____

From https://www.un.org/sustainabledevelopment, ©2019 United Nations. Used with the permission of the United Nations.

On the UN's website, take an in-depth look at the current situation with SDG #4:

QUALITY EDUCATION

Which fact or figure concerns you the most?

_____
_____
_____

Which target will address this concern?

_____
_____
_____

Use the space below to develop a plan to support this target.

What can you do in your school or local community?

How will courage come in handy when you carry out this plan?

_____

From https://www.un.org/sustainabledevelopment, ©2019 United Nations. Used with the permission of the United Nations.

Matchmaking

Look closely at these children and then choose 2 kids for each row in the chart below.

Description	Person 1	Person 2
Friends with one another		
Enemies with one another		
Friends with you		
Enemies with you		
Nice		
Not Nice		
Smart		
Not smart		
Cool		
Not cool		

Look at all the children in the green rows. Do they have anything in common?

_____

Look at all the children in the red rows. Do they have anything in common?

_____

We sometimes think negatively about things we just don't know much about. Might there be something more you could learn about the people in the red rows?

_____

HSS: Societal Structure and Culture

Nice To Meet You

Martin Luther King Jr. once said,

"Men often hate each other because they fear each other; | they fear each other because they don't know each other; | they don't know each other because they can not communicate; | they can not communicate because they are separated."

We are sometimes scared to make friends with certain people we don't know. Think of someone who you don't know very well at all, but are still for some reason scared or reluctant to be friends with. Do not name this person or write about anyone on this page, but rather think about the quote above and answer the following questions.

What don't you know about this person that might make you feel uncomfortable?
_____
_____

Do you communicate with this person? If so, describe how you communicate. If you don't communicate, explain why you don't or can't do this.
_____
_____

Are you somehow separated from this person? If so, how? _____
_____

Without mentioning this page, try to communicate better with this person. Find out more about this person by spending time together. Might you become friends? Reflect on the experience below.
_____
_____

Courageous

A Series of Fortunate Events

Label this timeline with events that shaped your level of courage. For any grades you're not in yet, label things you hope will happen or fear might happen which will in any case make you more courageous. Events might include making new friends, losing old friends, fights, challenges, grades, wins, losses, trouble, triumph, adventures, or mysteries.

KINDERGARTEN

GRADE 1

GRADE 2

GRADE 3

GRADE 4

GRADE 5

HSS: Time, Continuity, and Change

Tearing Down Walls

Choose someone you know whose courage tore down walls to make change and shape the world in which you live today. It may be a famous political activist who helped to change biased laws in your country, or it may be a kid on your school's student council who advocated for an improved school lunch menu. Research about or interview this person in order to answer the questions below.

Name: _____

Role in society: _____

Description of situation this individual intervened in: _____
_____
_____

What this individual wanted to change: _____
_____

Acts of courage this individual performed in order to make change: _____
_____

Description of situation after this individual intervened: _____
_____
_____

Description of how the situation would be if this individual had not changed things:
_____
_____
_____

MAP OF MY TOWN

Draw a map of your town and label as many places as you can, such as restaurants, shops, playgrounds, parks, rivers, lakes, forests, businesses, schools, streets, etc. Which areas have you never been to? Go out and explore these areas and continue to develop this map while you get to know your home better. Remember to stay safe on your travels!

HEROES OF MY TOWN

Research the history of your town and fill in the information below.

What did the area look like before it was inhabited? Draw a part of this environment that could have been intimidating.

Who were the first people to settle here? Where did they come from and why did they choose this location?

What were some of the challenges people faced when settling here? Rate how scary each obstacle was on a scale of 1-10.

Describe how people overcame each of these obstacles. Mention 2 specific people who were particularly courageous.

Courageous

WHY THE WASTE?

Be a risk-taker and change your habits to conserve resources.

Are your school snacks packaged in paper or plastic? What snacks could you bring that don't use as much packaging? Try these new foods as your snack for a week and reflect on how much material you've conserved.

PACKAGING

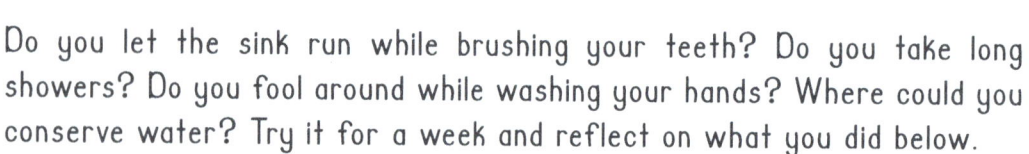

Do you let the sink run while brushing your teeth? Do you take long showers? Do you fool around while washing your hands? Where could you conserve water? Try it for a week and reflect on what you did below.

Water

Do you leave the lights or television on in a room that you leave? Do you use several devices that need to be charged? How could you reduce the amount of electricity you use? Reflect on your accomplishments below.

Electricity

Paper, ~~Rock~~ Markers, ~~Scissors~~ Tape

Your Limited Resources

While working in a group, create a series of 10 posters to hang around your school, each of which describes one way students can become even more courageous.

10 pieces of paper

6 inches of tape

1 package of markers

Develop a plan that details when group members will use which materials in order to produce the best quality products in the least amount of time. Then follow your plan and create your posters with your group. Afterward reflect on how you distributed your resources to your partners. Was anyone left out? Was the plan efficient? Did another group in your class have a better plan? Use the space below to plan and reflect.

PLAN

REFLECT

ECUADOR

Ecuador is a wonderful place known for its incredible natural beauty, splendid cultural influence and admirable people. But like everywhere else in the world, the geographical elements can present challenges to those who live there. Research some of the geographical elements below and determine whether any of them can be challenging. Then write a short narrative on the lines below describing how people living in Ecuador might need courage when handling these geographical elements.

- Landforms
- Landscape
- Wildlife
- Weather
- Natural Disasters
- Climate
- Topography

Fairtrade Bananas

Some banana farmers in Ecuador suffer from poor wages, unsuitable housing, long work days, no job security, and child labor. Stand up for these farmers and use this page to design a creative way to spread awareness of unethical banana production. Look up the Fairtrade Foundation website in your country to find out ways you can support banana farmers around the world, or consider some of the ideas below.

ALWAYS BUY tHe BANANAS WItH tHe Fairtrade MarK!

give an informative presentation at an assembly. Ask local grocery stores to sell Fairtrade bananas only. Hold a banana bread bake sale and donate your proceeds to support banana farmers.

Design a monkey mascot and put it on posters, brochures, or a website. Dress up like a banana and

Create banana peel hats and wear them to school with a sign that says "Ask me why I'm wearing a banana peel on my head," and then tell everyone why!

HSS Reflection

1 How does this chapter connect to another chapter you've engaged with so far?

2 Which page was most difficult for you to complete? What was hard about it?

3 How would you rate the quality of your work in this chapter, from 1 (Yikes!) to 10 (Wow!), and why?

TECHNOLOGY

1 Hardware and Appliances
devices, personification, operation, instructions

2 Software and Applications
programs, discovery, WeVideo, functions

3 Internet
clickbait, pop-ups, websites, keywords

4 Digital Citizenship
cyberbullying, responsibility, fair use, copyright

HOUSEHOLD HEROES

Explore your home and choose a device or appliance to personify (which means to give a non-human thing human characteristics). Learn how the machine's parts work together to accomplish its purpose (either online, in a book, or physically with the help of an adult). Write a story about how courageous this device is when it does its job. Perhaps it's the brave blender who battles acidic juices, or the spirited space heater whose coils protect bare feet on chilly nights!

_____
_____
_____
_____
_____
_____
_____
_____
_____
_____
_____
_____
_____
_____
_____

List all the devices you know how to operate in your home.

_____   _____
_____   _____
_____   _____
_____   _____

Labeled Diagram

Grasping New Gadgets

Explore other appliances around your home and ask your parent to show you how to operate something you've never used before. Draw a diagram of the device, labeling all parts, buttons, and cables. Then write a list of step by step instructions on how to operate this device so you don't forget! And always remember, safety first!

Instructions

_____
_____
_____
_____
_____
_____
_____
_____
_____
_____
_____
_____
_____
_____
_____

Pesky Programs

Be a risk-taker and explore a software program that you've always been interested in but found too difficult to understand. Then just play around and see what you can discover and learn!

Name of software: _____

Why it was intimidating: _____

The first thing you explored in this software: _____

Three things you learned about this software:

1. _____

2. _____

3. _____

Two things you don't know how to do but want to learn:

1. _____

2. _____

Your plan for learning how to do these 2 things: _____
_____
_____

Valiant Video

Visit the website **www.wevideo.com** and sign up for a free account.

Once you're logged in, go to **DASHBOARD** and then **Create+ New** to create a new video.

Play around for a while and explore the different functions. Then browse through the 6 main folders and search for elements within those folders that you feel represent courage the most.

ESSENTIALS LIBRARY

Name of Media: _____

How it shows courage: _____
_____

MEDIA

You probably don't have any media imported yet. Record some footage of a courageous moment and then upload it here.

TEXT

Name of Media: _____

How it shows courage: _____
_____

AUDIO

Name of Media: _____

How it shows courage: _____
_____

TRANSITIONS

Name of Media: _____

How it shows courage: _____
_____

GRAPHICS

Name of Media: _____

How it shows courage: _____
_____

Clickbait

Ads pop up on many websites that we visit. Clicking on these pop-ups may lead to impulse-purchasing, computer viruses, unwanted sharing of private information, or pathways to inappropriate web pages. How can we avoid falling into the traps of clickbait?

Surf the web for a while and collect information on all of the advertisements, email requests, and "Congratulations, you're a winner" announcements that pop up on your pages.

What kinds of products and services are advertised? _____
_____

What techniques do the advertisers use with these pop-ups? Consider colors, sounds, animation, flashing, screen position, images, fonts and persuasive techniques explained on p. 29 in this book.
_____
_____
_____

How might some of these techniques intimidate or force people to click on them?
_____
_____

What are some strategies you could use and share with others to help everyone avoid being tricked or bullied into falling for clickbait?
_____
_____

Keywords and Phrases

Find 6 websites that help people understand what it means to be courageous. Begin by writing down some keywords and phrases to enter into a search engine. Depending on these keywords and phrases, the sites that come up will be different. Keep these phrases short and specific. Beneath each phrase you use, write down the url for each of the first 3 websites listed.

Keywords or Phrase
_____

www._____

www._____

www._____

Keywords or Phrase
_____

www._____

www._____

www._____

Which keywords or phrase resulted in the better set of websites for what you were searching for?
_____

Choose the website you feel is best for teaching people about being courageous. Summarize the website below and provide reasons for why you would recommend this website to someone else.

www._____

Summary:_____
_____
_____

Recommendation:_____
_____

Report Cyberbullying!

You may have seen cyberbullying in online games and chat rooms or on social media. The next time you see cyberbullying, do not ignore it! Take action and say something. Tell a teacher, your parents or another responsible adult. Report abuse to the system's administration, and even say something to the cyberbully if you feel safe doing so. The important thing is to be courageous and do something about it. No one has the right to bully anyone, in any form.

Document details below the next time your observe cyberbullying.

System or program where cyberbullying was observed: _____

Date occurred: _____

Cyberbully's name or username: _____

Victim's name or username: _____

Text or description of cyberbullying: _____

_____

_____

Responsible adults informed: _____

How and when they were informed: _____

Actions taken by anyone to prevent specific cyberbully from abusing others again: _____

_____

_____

Fair Use vs. Copyright

Many images, texts, and videos that you find online are protected under copyright by their creators. Review some of the projects and presentations you've made in the past where you included text or graphics you found on the internet. (This means that picture you found on Google Images that you printed and glued onto a poster.) Go back online and find one of these items. Then draft an email to the owner below, requesting permission to use this piece of work.

Description of item (text, graphic, video, etc.): _____

_____

Uniform Resource Locator (url, or web address): _____

Source / Owner: _____

Source / Owner contact information: _____

Description of your project: _____

_____

Reasons why you want this item: _____

_____

Rough draft of email: _____

_____

_____

_____

_____

Technology Reflection

1 Which page would you like to share with your family or class? Why?

2 Which resources did you use while engaging with this chapter? Did they help or cause complications?

3 How would you improve one of the activities included in this chapter?

Multiple Intelligences

1. **Verbal-linguistic**
   poems, stories, speeches, commercials

2. **Mathematical-logical**
   surveys, statistics, lists, causes and effects

3. **Visual-spatial**
   collages, photographs, maps, comics

4. **Musical**
   songs, instruments, sound effects, genres

5. **Bodily-kinesthetic**
   handshakes, postures, sports, dances

6. **Intrapersonal**
   autobiographies, mirrors, protagonists, scrapbooks

7. **Interpersonal**
   friends, interviews, skits, competitions

8. **Naturalist**
   animals, plants, seasons, environments

9. **Existential**
   twins, other worlds, doors to dimensions, destinies

Verbal-Linguistic Menu

Write a polite letter to a bully requesting him or her to be more friendly.

Author a story about a character who is particularly courageous, or not courageous at all!

Create a pack of vocabulary flash cards with the definitions of synonyms and antonyms for the word courageous!

Create a newspaper or magazine with articles that cover different stories about courage.

Prepare a speech about how to be courageous and share it in class or at an assembly.

Record a radio program or commercial covering the idea of courage.

Write a poem about courage, such as a haiku, acrostic, or limmerick.

Write a theater play that focuses on courage. Plan and perform the play in front of your class!

Create a crossword puzzle or word search using nouns and verbs that connect to courage.

My Verbal-Linguistic Selection

Complete an activity from the menu and share what you learned about courage from this experience. You might write a summary, draw a picture, sketch a storyboard, or choose another way to present your findings.

Mathematical-Logical Menu

Make a list of your problems and order them from the least to greatest amount of courage it takes to solve them.

Survey your classmates about how courageous they feel on a scale of 1-10. Analyze the mean, median, and mode.

Tally signs of courage from others on the playground and conclude which days/times courage happens most often.

Analyze your most courageous and most nervous moments to identify factors that cause these.

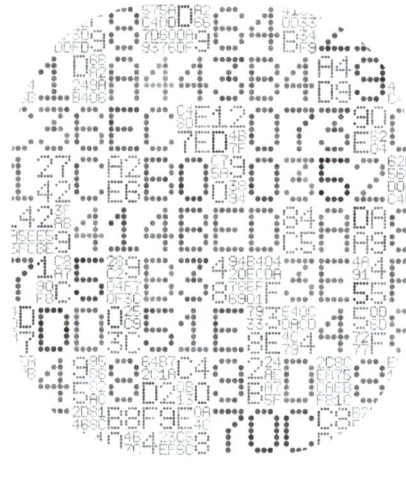

Create a secret code for courageous messages using numbers, letters, or symbols.

Interview others about their fearful moments to determine and analyze trends in causes of fears.

Imagine your toys at home are alive and organize them by levels of courage.

Using the scientific method, design an experiment that could test a question about measuring courage or fear.

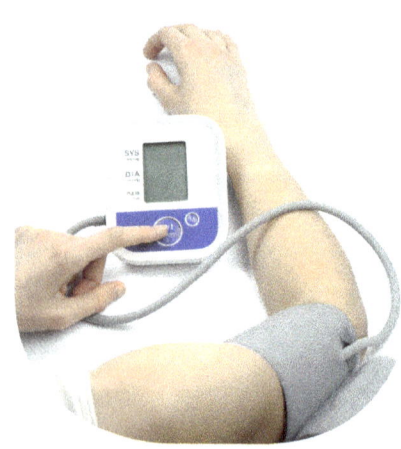

Chart your blood pressure before and after trying new things like eating new foods or meeting new people.

My Mathematical-Logical Selection

Complete an activity from the menu and share what you learned about courage from this experience. You might write a summary, draw a picture, sketch a storyboard, or choose another way to present your findings.

Visual-Spatial Menu

Organize a collage of courageous pictures you find in old magazines and newspapers.

Take artistic photographs of courageous people you see around you.

Design a symbol or logo that stands for fear and cross it out.

Invent a place called Courageous Island and make a map of it.

Draw a courageous illustration and then cut it into pieces to play with as a jigsaw puzzle.

Redesign the cover of this book.

Paint an abstract painting of courage.

Create a comic strip depicting brave characters or telling a story about brave moments in your life.

Experiment with new media and choose an art form that you feel represents courage the best.

My Visual-Spatial Selection

Complete an activity from the menu and share what you learned about courage from this experience. You might write a summary, draw a picture, sketch a storyboard, or choose another way to present your findings.

Musical Menu

Choose one of your favorite songs and rewrite the lyrics to include messages about courage.

Find a story or poem about courage and set it to your own music.

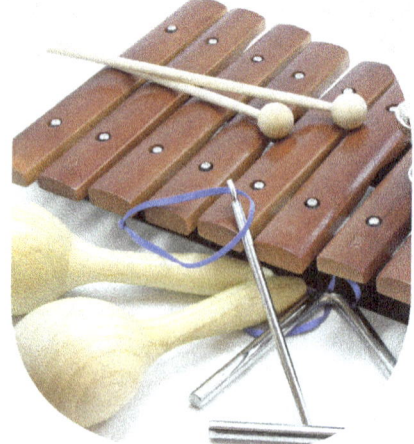

Experiment with different instruments and determine which one produces the best courageous notes.

Write your own courageous musical composition.

Explore how an element of music might be used to add courage to a piece (rhythm, dynamics, tempo, form, melody, harmony).

Sing a song about courage in front of a live audience.

Write and perform a rap about overcoming fears and anxiety.

Listen to different music genres and determine how different styles portray courage in different ways.

Record sound effects of everyday objects and determine which ones are most courageous and/or most fearful.

My Musical Selection

Complete an activity from the menu and share what you learned about courage from this experience. You might write a summary, draw a picture, sketch a storyboard, or choose another way to present your findings.

Bodily-Kinesthetic Menu

Collect and photograph a variety of courageous facial expressions.

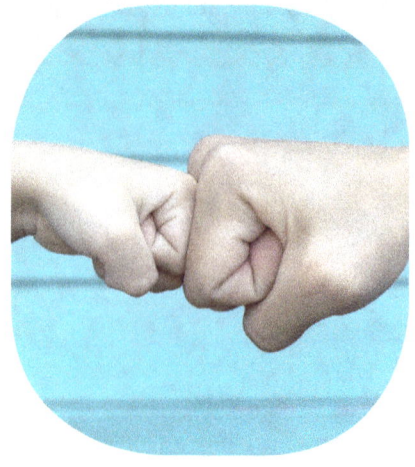

Invent a secret handshake that will pump you up before you're about to do something courageous.

Create different yoga poses that symbolize courage to help drive fear from your body.

Make a collage or video montage of brave moments in sports.

Invent a new sport where players earn points for showing courage.

Play charades and act out moments of challenge and courage.

Learn different cultural dances that celebrate bravery.

Create an exercise routine that will warm you up before you want to do something that makes you nervous.

Design a courageous costume, mask, or uniform and try it on for size.

My Bodily-Kinesthetic Selection

Complete an activity from the menu and share what you learned about courage from this experience. You might write a summary, draw a picture, sketch a storyboard, or choose another way to present your findings.

Intrapersonal Menu

Write an autobiography highlighting your bravest moments, and include a chapter that happens in the future.

Look in the mirror and draw a self-portrait that highlights the bravery in your eyes and facial expression.

Find a quiet place to talk to yourself, admitting your fears and complimenting your courage.

Make graphs that record data about your courageous moments or your fears.

Choose a character from a movie who you admire and compare and contrast yourself to him or her.

Make a list of things that make you nervous and develop goals to help you overcome these fears.

Rewrite a story and add yourself as a hero who saves the day!

Create a scrapbook of your bravest moments with images, words, or objects that remind you of these moments.

Make a timeline of all the challenging moments in your life that took courage for you to overcome.

My Intrapersonal Selection

Complete an activity from the menu and share what you learned about courage from this experience. You might write a summary, draw a picture, sketch a storyboard, or choose another way to present your findings.

Interpersonal Menu

Invent a board game that requires players to show courage, and then play it with your friends!

Visit classrooms of younger students and present a pep talk about being courageous.

Explore new friendships with older students you admire but have never approached before.

Interview others to get their perspectives on what it means to be brave or stories about courage.

Organize a friendly competition to see who's the most courageous in your class.

Play with someone new until you've had quality playing time with every single classmate.

Create a play or puppet show and perform it in front of a live audience.

Organize a group of friends to help younger students when they're nervous or afraid.

Teach a lesson on how to become even more courageous to your classmates.

My Interpersonal Selection

Complete an activity from the menu and share what you learned about courage from this experience. You might write a summary, draw a picture, sketch a storyboard, or choose another way to present your findings.

Naturalist Menu

List the various natural environments near you. Explain which one is best for a brave adventure.

Collect objects from nature that symbolize courage and make a collage.

Nominate winners for the Most Courageous Animal, Plant, Land Formation etc. and explain why they win.

Engage with an animal you're afraid of, or learn more about it to discover its respectable qualities.

Decide which of the 4 seasons requires the most courage from plants and animals.

Create a project that honors a migratory species which needs courage to overcome challenges on its journey.

Explore an area of nature that you've never been to before.

Write a field trip proposal to your teachers explaining how nature makes children more courageous.

Take pictures of moments where nature looks brave, and create a collage or digital presentation.

My Naturalist Selection

Complete an activity from the menu and share what you learned about courage from this experience. You might write a summary, draw a picture, sketch a storyboard, or choose another way to present your findings.

Existential Menu

Create a story about how artificial intelligence would need courage under specific circumstances.

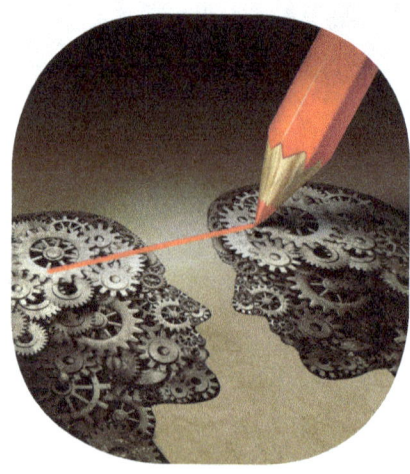

Experiment to determine if courageous thoughts can be communicated via the theory of telepathy.

If there were doors to other dimensions, show how you could use them to advance your courageous approaches to life.

Harness your courage to defend your theory of how the universe came to be.

Construct a series of events that would require the most courage and explain how to handle them if people could time travel.

Write a conversation you would have with your twin from a parallel universe if you discussed life courage.

Explain how choosing your own destiny requires great courage.

Write a new World Turtle mytheme about a creature carrying the world along a courageous journey.

Design another world where different kinds of beings display courage in a different way than what we know.

My Existential Selection

Complete an activity from the menu and share what you learned about courage from this experience. You might write a summary, draw a picture, sketch a storyboard, or choose another way to present your findings.

Courageous

Multiple Intelligences Reflection

1. How does your preferred intelligence influence how courageous you are?

2. Which intelligence did you connect the least with? Why do you feel this way?

3. If you could select a different activity from a menu to complete, which would it be and why?

Reflections And Wrap-Ups

1 Congratulations!
praise, instructions, addresses, call to action

2 Doodle Diary
thoughts, drawings, speech bubbles, comic frames

3 Grand Reflection
looking back, looking forward, review, consideration

4 Letters to the Stars
communication, pen pals, Star Character Name, email

Congratulations!

We hope you feel more courageous in many different ways after completing some of these activities! After all your hard work and achievements as a responsible risk-taker, you must have some stories to tell! Please send us your tales of courage, words of wisdom, or even photos, scans or photocopies of your best pages in this portfolio! We'd be happy to share your experiences on our website and social media channels so other children around the world can be inspired by the ways in which you have become even more courageous!

Your Grand Reflection is Awaiting!

Hopefully your Doodle Diary is full of thoughts, scribbles, ideas, rants and cheers!

Blast us an email!

StarCharacterSeries@gmail.com

Write to us!

Star Character Series
Postfach 131
67247 Freinsheim
Germany

Until next time, take care and be courageous!

Grand

Which page did you complete first? Last? Compare these 2 pages. Is there a difference in the quality of the work you did, or how you approached the tasks?

_____
_____
_____
_____

What was the most surprising thing you learned about yourself when completing these activities?

_____
_____
_____
_____

Looking forward, how will you continue to develop and grow as a courageous individual? What kinds of actions will you take?

_____
_____
_____
_____

Reflection

Did you achieve the goals you set out to accomplish on page 5? Explain how you managed to achieve them or why they didn't work out.

_____

Which page best represents your personal level of courage? How does this activity reveal this?

_____

Which activity in this book challenged your courage the most? How did you overcome any intimidation?

_____

Email to the Stars

Use the open New Message email below to plan an email to us! It might be an exciting story about one of the courageous activities you completed in this book, or maybe you want to share some advice with other kids around the world about what it means to become even more courageous.

We can't post your real name, so if you'd like the chance to see your stories or ideas shared, include your made-up Star Character Name and we'll give you a shoutout!

Your Star Character Name: _____

New Message   _ ▢ ✕

To   StarCharacterSeries@gmail.com

Subject

Don't forget to include your Star Character Name in your email!

Letter to the Stars

Pen pal letters are just as fun as emails! Mail your letter to

Star Character Series
Postfach 131
67247 Freinsheim
Germany

Join in the fun!

Follow us for news, entertainment, shoutouts, new releases, and more!

Just search for **Star Character Series** on your favorite social media channels!

To place an order, please visit our website!
www.LivandBluePublishing.com

For discounts on class sets, please email us!
livandbluepublishing@gmail.com

MEET ALL MY FRIENDS IN THE STAR CHARACTER SERIES!

INQUIRING

CARING

KNOWLEDGEABLE

THOUGHTFUL

COMMUNICATIVE

PRINCIPLED

OPEN-MINDED

BALANCED

REFLECTIVE

www.ingramcontent.com/pod-product-compliance
Lightning Source LLC
Chambersburg PA
CBHW081103070526
44584CB00021B/3181